P9-CDW-101

WILDFLOWERS
OF THE GREAT LAKES REGION

WILDFLOWERS
OF THE GREAT LAKES REGION

Written and Illustrated by
Roberta L. Simonds and Henrietta H. Tweedie

CHICAGO REVIEW PRESS

Chicago

This book is dedicated to our husbands, Richard and Edwin, for their loving support, and to our talented and enthusiastic teacher of botanical illustration, Nancy Hart, staff artist of the Morton Arboretum. We also wish to thank Ray Schulenberg, of the Morton Arboretum, for his help in identifying and correcting many of our drawings, and our children and friends for their interest and encouragement.

Copyright ©1978 by Henrietta H. Tweedie and Roberta L. Simonds
Second edition first printing 1983
All rights reserved
ISBN 0-914091-45-X
Chicago Review Press, 213 W. Institute Place, Chicago

INTRODUCTION

The wild flowers of the woods and roadsides of the Great Lakes region are enjoyed by summer visitors and year round residents alike. Their color and variety soon intrigue even the casual viewer. Everyone recognizes some wild flowers such as dandelions, violets, daisies, and roses, but beyond these we need help if we are to call them by name. This book will aid beginners to identify the more common local wild flowers. Although we drew these flowers in the lake counties of western Michigan during our many wonderful summer vacations, most of them grow in northern Illinois, northern Indiana, Wisconsin, eastern Michigan, and the upper peninsula.

There are two kinds of wild flowers—native, and old world or alien. These old world flowers came into the country mixed in the seed bags and stuck in the mud on the boots of pioneers. Their women carried packets of seeds in their pockets to plant reminders of home. Winter Cress, Chicory, and Queen Anne's Lace are examples. These flowers will grow in poor disturbed soil, rapidly covering scars of building and erosion with colorful blooms. They withstand air pollution, traffic, and even the mower. We see these vigorous plants from our cars as we whiz down the freeway or meander along a sandy road. While most old world flowers are annuals, many of our native plants are perennials with deep roots which survive drought and fire, but are vulnerable to the bulldozer and plow. Native plants tend to be less conspicuous and less numerous than the aliens, and today are mostly found in undisturbed woods, ravines, fence rows, and on riverbanks—habitats to which man has limited access. Native orchids are so rare now that their dwelling places should be kept secret. Trilliums, however, still whiten spring woods, while clumps of bright orange Butterfly-Weed decorate the roadsides, and Cardinal Flowers on riverbanks delight the canoeist and fisherman.

We have grouped the flowers by seasons—spring, summer, and fall—and in each group by habitat. We have used for reference the *New Britton and Brown Illustrated Flora of Northeastern United States and Adjacent Canada,* Fifth Edition, New York, 1974.

Roberta L. Simonds
Henrietta H. Tweedie

Spring comes to the Great Lakes region in early April when Skunk Cabbage pushes its way through the snow. As the Harbinger-of-Spring lifts its salt and pepper blossoms above last fall's decaying leaves, the beech and maple forests turn silver, green and gold. Pine and Hemlock trees are tipped with new green needles and roadsides and fields are yellow with Winter Cress. The sky is filled with migrating birds.

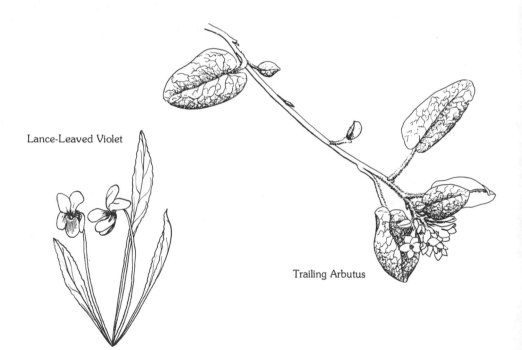

Lance-Leaved Violet

Trailing Arbutus

LANCE-LEAVED VIOLET *Viola lanceolata.* Violet family *Violaceae.* Spring.
Flowers white. Leaves smooth, slender, long and tapering. Height 2-6 inches. Bogs, streambanks, and swamps.

TRAILING ARBUTUS *Epigaea repens.* Heath family *Ericaceae.* Spring.
Flowers pink to white, fragrant. Leaves alternate, leathery, on creeping woody stems. Height 6-8 inches. Woods.

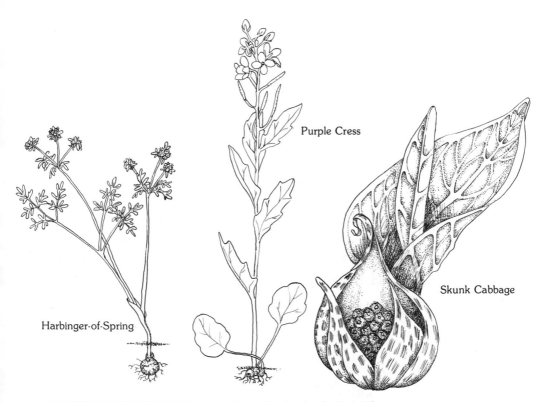

Purple Cress

Skunk Cabbage

Harbinger-of-Spring

HARBINGER-OF-SPRING *Erigenia bulbosa*. Parsley family *Umbelliferae*.
  Flowers white petals, black stamens. Height 4-9 inches. Wet woods.

PURPLE CRESS *Cardamine douglassi*. Mustard family *Cruciferae*.
  Flowers pink. Round basal leaves. Height 8-20 inches. Wet woods.

SKUNK CABBAGE *Symplocarpus foetidus*. Arum family *Araceae*.
  Flowers on a round spadix inside a mottled green and brown spathe. Leaves open later
  becoming very large and bright green. Height 1-3 feet. Wet woods.

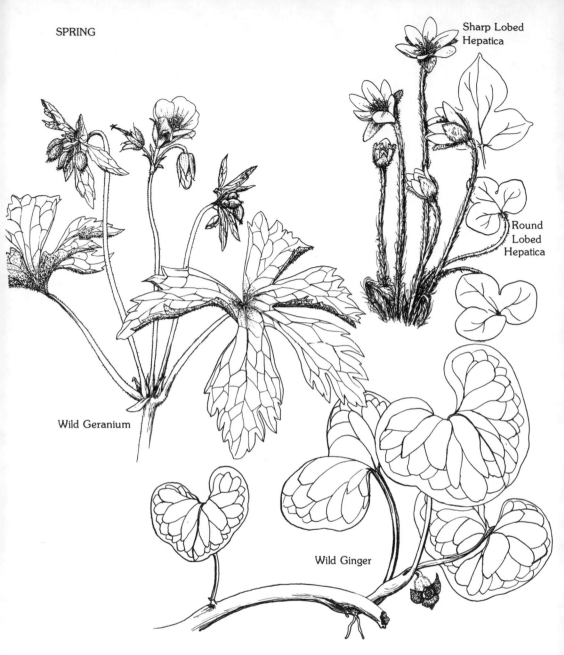

Sharp Lobed Hepatica

Round Lobed Hepatica

Wild Geranium

Wild Ginger

WILD GERANIUM, CRANE'S BILL *Geranium maculatum.* Geranium family *Geraniaceae.*
   Flowers rose-purple, seed has a sharp point like a beak. Height 1-2 feet. Woods.

HEPATICA, SHARP LOBED *Hepatica acutiloba.* Buttercup family *Ranunculaceae.*
   Flowers white, pink, lavender, appear before the leaves. Stems very hairy. Height 4-9 inches.
   Woods.

HEPATICA, ROUND LOBED *Hepatica americana.* Buttercup family *Ranunculaceae.*
   Same as above but leaves have rounded tips.

WILD GINGER *Asarum canadense.* Birthwort family *Aristolochiaceae.*
   Flowers dark red, cup shaped and hidden by heart shaped leaves. Height 6-12 inches. Woods.

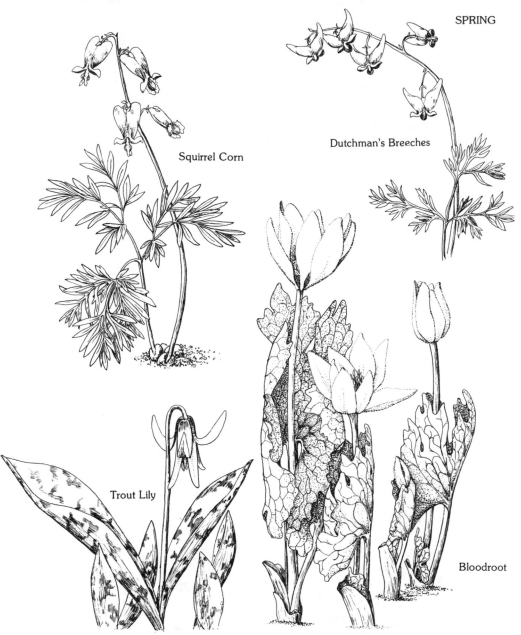

Squirrel Corn

Dutchman's Breeches

Trout Lily

Bloodroot

BLOODROOT *Sanguinaria canadensis.* Poppy family *Papaveraceae.*
Flowers white, surrounded by the leaf when in bud. Red juice. Height 6-12 inches. Rich woods.

TROUT LILY, DOGTOOTH VIOLET *Erythronium americanum.* Lily family *Liliaceae.*
Flowers yellow, leaves spotted like trout. Grows in large colonies. Height 5-10 inches. Rich woods.

SQUIRREL CORN *Dicentra canadensis.* Fumitory family *Fumariaceae.*
Flowers white, an inflated "bleeding heart" shape. Tubers like small peas. Height up to 10 inches. Rich woods.

DUTCHMAN'S BREECHES *Dicentra cucullaria.* Fumitory family *Fumariaceae.*
Flowers white, similar to Squirrel Corn but elongated into "breeches". Height up to 10 inches. Rich woods.

9

Solomon's Seal

Solomon's
Plume

Starry Solomon's Seal

SOLOMON'S SEAL *Polygonatum canaliculatum.* Lily family *Liliaceae.*
  Flowers greenish-white along stem, berries dark blue. Height 1-3 feet. Woods.

STARRY SOLOMON'S SEAL *Smilacina stellata.* Lily family *Liliaceae.*
  Flowers white at top of erect plant. Berries red speckled with purple. Height 1-2 feet. Woods.

SOLOMON'S PLUME *Smilacina racemosa.* Lily family *Liliaceae.*
  Flowers a white cluster at top of stem. Berries black or green with black stripes. Height 1-3 feet.
  Woods.

Nodding Trillium

Great White Trillium

Wake Robin

GREAT WHITE TRILLIUM *Trillium grandiflorum.* Lily family *Liliaceae.*
  Flowers 3 white petals, fading to pink, 3 large leaves. Height 12-18 inches. Rich, moist woods.

NODDING TRILLIUM *Trillium cernuum.* Lily family *Liliaceae.*
  Flowers 3 white petals nod below the 3 leaves. Height 8-16 inches. Rich, moist woods.

WAKE ROBIN, RED TRILLIUM *Trillium recurvatum.* Lily family *Liliaceae.*
  Flowers dark red. Petals close together just above 3 mottled leaves. Height 7-16 inches. Moist woods.

Spring Beauty

Two-leaved Toothwort

Cut-leaved Toothwort

TWO-LEAVED TOOTHWORT, CRINKLEROOT *Dentaria diphylla*. Mustard family *Cruciferae*.
Flowers white, upper leaves nearly opposite. Height 12-18 inches. Woods.

CUT-LEAVED TOOTHWORT *Dentaria laciniata*. Mustard family *Cruciferae*.
Flowers white, 3 deeply cut leaves in a whorl. Height 8-15 inches. Woods.

SPRING BEAUTY *Claytonia virginica*. Purslane family *Portulacaceae*.
Flowers white with pink veins, leaves fleshy. Height 6-12 inches. Open woods and clearnings.

Bishop's Cap

Foam Flower

Green Dragon

BISHOP'S CAP, MITERWORT *Mitella diphylla*. Saxifrage family *Saxifragaceae*.
Flowers tiny, white, with fringed petals. Height 8-16 inches. Rich woods.

GREEN DRAGON *Arisaema dracontium*. Arum family *Araceae*.
Flowers on long green spadix, extends beyond narrow pointed spathe. Height 1-4 feet. Rich woods.

FOAM FLOWER *Tiarella cordifolia*. Saxifrage family *Saxifragaceae*.
Flowers white on leafless stem. Height 6-12 inches. Rich woods.

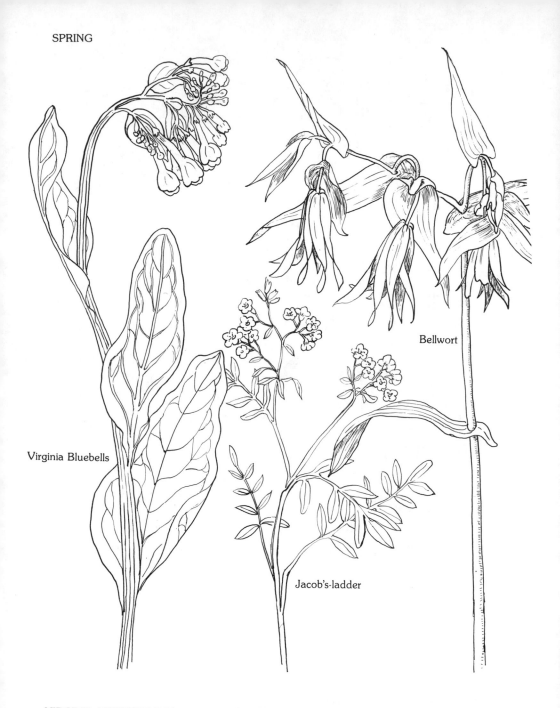

Virginia Bluebells

Bellwort

Jacob's-ladder

VIRGINIA BLUEBELLS *Mertensia virginica.* Borage family *Boraginaceae.*
Flowers blue, buds pink, nodding. Stem smooth. Height 1-2 feet. River bottoms and woods.

JACOB'S-LADDER *Polemonium reptans.* Phlox family *Polemoniaceae.*
Flowers blue, paired leaflets form ladder. Height 1-2 feet. Wet woods.

BELLWORT *Uvularia grandiflora.* Lily family *Lilaceae.*
Flowers yellow, bell-like; stems pierce the leaves. Height 6-20 inches. Rich woods.

May Apple

Cinquefoil

Wild Strawberry

MAY APPLE, MANDRAKE *Podophyllum peltatum.* Barberry family *Berberidaceae.*
  Flowers single, nodding, waxy, white. Large deeply divided leaves. Height 12-18 inches.
  Colonies in open woods, roadsides.

WILD STRAWBERRY *Fragaria virginiana.* Rose family *Rosaceae.*
  Flowers white, yellow centers. Leaves 3 parted. Hairy plants send out runners to form colonies.
  Delicious red fruit. Height 3-6 inches. Fields, open places.

CINQUEFOIL *Potentilla simplex.* Rose family *Rosaceae.*
  Flowers yellow, leaves have 5 fingers. Height 1-3 feet. Grows by runners. Common in dry open
  woods and fields.

Early Meadow Rue

Columbine

EARLY MEADOW RUE *Thalictrum dioicum.* Buttercup family *Ranunculaceae.*
 Flowers greenish, unisexual, in graceful panicles. Airy light green foliage. Height 1-2 feet.
 Woods.

COLUMBINE *Aquilegia canadensis.* Buttercup family *Ranunculaceae.*
 Flowers scarlet and yellow, nodding at top of plant. Height 2-3 feet. Woods.

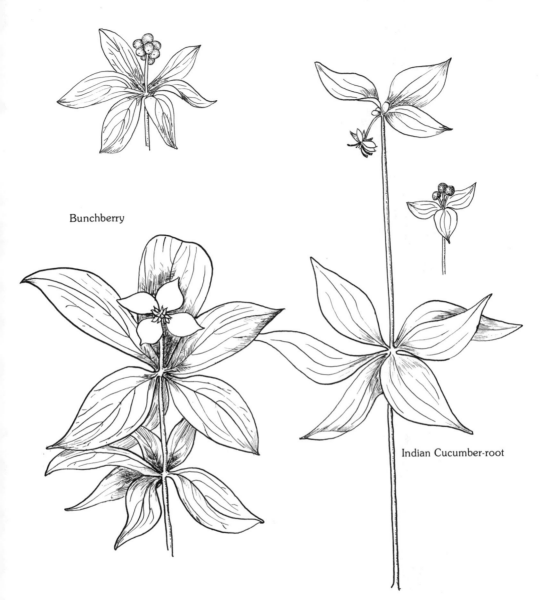

Bunchberry

Indian Cucumber-root

BUNCHBERRY *Cornus canadensis.* Dogwood family *Cornaceae.*
  Flowers white, berries bright red. Often grows in colonies. Height 12-18 inches. Woods.

INDIAN CUCUMBER-ROOT *Medeola virginiana.* Lily family *Liliaceae.*
  Flowers greenish-yellow, upright berries blue. Leaves in 2 whorls. Height 1-3 feet. Woods.

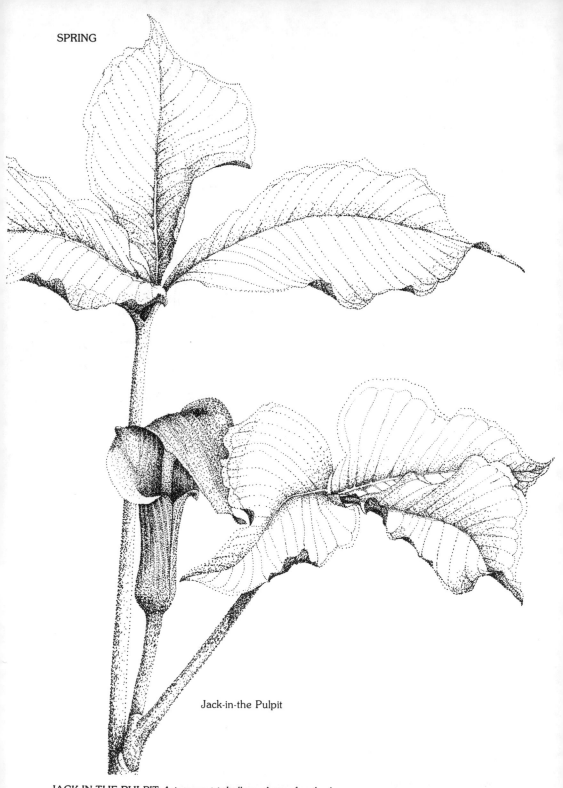

Jack-in-the Pulpit

JACK-IN-THE-PULPIT *Arisaema triphyllum*. Arum family *Araceae*.
Flowers on spadix with long spathe bending over. Leaf 3 parted. Height 1-3 feet. Wet woods.

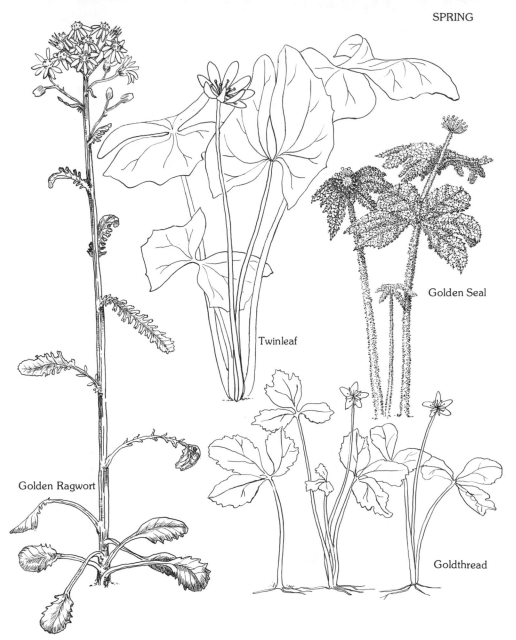

Golden Seal

Twinleaf

Golden Ragwort

Goldthread

GOLDEN RAGWORT *Senecio aureus*. Daisy family *Compositae*.
 Flowers yellow. Height 1-3 feet. Wet woods, swampy places.

GOLDTHREAD *Coptis trifolia*. Buttercup family *Ranunculaceae*.
 Flowers white, leaves dark, shiny, evergreen. Height 3-6 inches. Wet woods, bogs.

TWINLEAF *Jeffersonia diphylla*. Barberry family *Berberidaceae*.
 Flowers white, leaves divided into two parts. Height 8-12 inches. Rich woods.

GOLDEN SEAL *Hydrastis canadensis*. Buttercup family *Ranunculaceae*.
 Flowers have no petals, many stamens and pistils, leaves dark and crinkled growing larger as
 flowers fade. Height 1-16 inches. Rich woods.

Rue Anemone

False Rue Anemone

Wood Anemone

WOOD ANEMONE *Anemone quinquefolia.* Buttercup family *Ranunculaceae.*
Flowers white, single and delicate. Height 4-8 inches. Woods.

RUE ANEMONE *Anemonella thalictroides.* Buttercup family *Ranunculaceae.*
Flowers white, delicate, always in motion, rising from a whorl of leaves. Height 4-10 inches.
Woods.

FALSE RUE ANEMONE *Isopyrum biternatum.* Buttercup family *Ranunculaceae.*
Flowers white, single from axils of leaves. Height 8-12 inches. Woods.

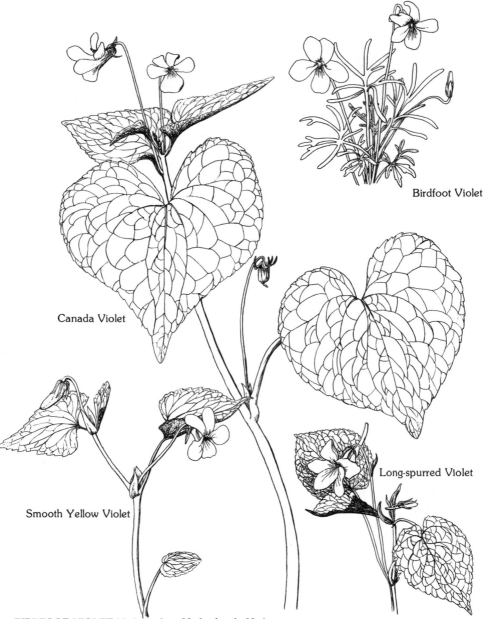

Birdfoot Violet

Canada Violet

Long-spurred Violet

Smooth Yellow Violet

BIRDFOOT VIOLET *Viola pedata.* Violet family *Violaceae.*
Flowers lilac, some bi-colored with top 2 petals dark blue. Leaves finely cut. Height 4-10 inches.
Dry sandy open woods and fields.

SMOOTH YELLOW VIOLET *Viola eriocarpa.* Violet family *Violaceae.*
Flowers yellow, stem and leaves smooth. Height 4-12 inches. Woods.

CANADA VIOLET *Viola canadensis.* Violet family *Violaceae.*
Flowers white, buds pink, fragrant. Height 8-16 inches. Woods.

LONG-SPURRED VIOLET *Viola rostrata.* Violet family *Violaceae.*
Flowers pale violet with long spur. Height 4-8 inches. Rich woods.

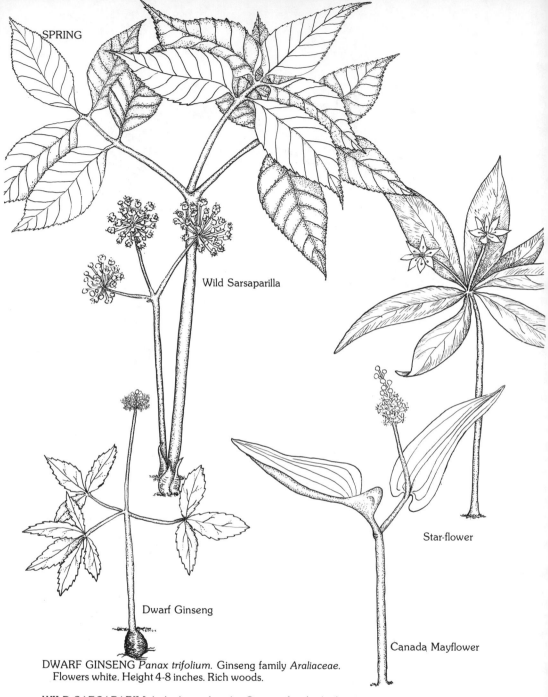

SPRING

Wild Sarsaparilla

Star-flower

Dwarf Ginseng

Canada Mayflower

DWARF GINSENG *Panax trifolium.* Ginseng family *Araliaceae.*
   Flowers white. Height 4-8 inches. Rich woods.

WILD SARSAPARILLA *Aralia nudicaulis.* Ginseng family *Araliaceae.*
   Flowers are white clusters on stem separate from leaves. Height 1-3 feet. Rich woods.

CANADA MAYFLOWER, WILD LILY-OF-THE-VALLEY *Maianthemum canadense.* Lily family
Liliaceae.
   Flowers white. Height 3-9 inches. Rich woods.

STAR-FLOWER *Trientalis borealis.* Primrose family *Primulaceae.*
   Flowers white, two 6-7 pointed stars above shiny leaves. Height 4-9 inches. Rich woods.

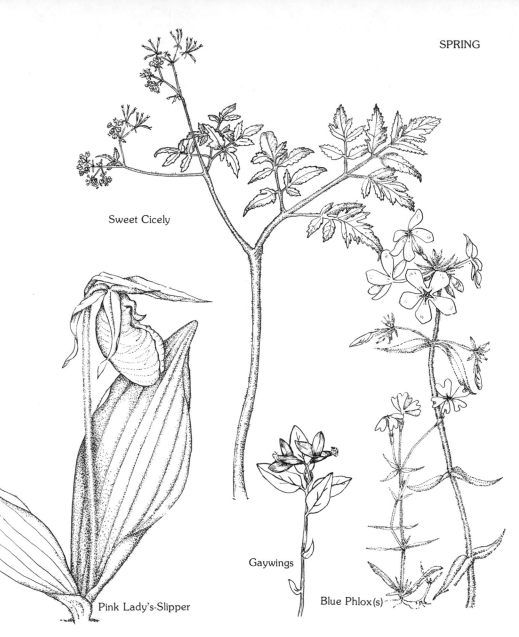

Sweet Cicely

Pink Lady's-Slipper

Gaywings

Blue Phlox(s)

PINK LADY'S-SLIPPER, **MOCCASIN** FLOWER *Cypripedium acaule.* Orchid family *Orchidaceae.*
Flowers pink to rose, 2 basal leaves. Height 12-18 inches. Dry or wet acid soil. Rare, protected.

SWEET CICELY *Osmorhiza claytoni.* Parsley family *Umbelliferae.*
Flowers white. Height 1½ to 3 feet. Woods.

GAYWINGS, FRINGED POLYGALA *Polygala paucifolia.* Milkwort family *Polygalaceae.*
Flowers red-purple, resemble orchids, yellow stamens, evergreen leaves. Height 3-6 inches.
Rich woods.

BLUE PHLOX *Phlox divaricata.* Phlox family *Polemoniaceae.*
Flowers pale blue. Height 10-20 inches. Rich open woods.

BLUE PHLOX *Phlox bifida.* Phlox family *Polemoniaceae.*
Flowers pale blue, petals notched. Height 2-8 inches. Sandy woods, rock ledges.

Blue Cohosh

White Baneberry

BLUE COHOSH *Caulophyllum thalictroides.* Barberry family *Berberiadaceae.*
Flowers greenish yellow, become blue berries. Height 1-3 feet. Woods.

WHITE BANEBERRY *Actaea pachypoda.* Buttercup family *Ranunculaceae.*
Flowers in a white spike, form white berries known as doll's eyes on thick red stalks. RED
BANEBERRY *Actea rubra* has red berries on thin stalks. Height 1-3 feet. Woods.

Blue-eyed Grass

Yellow Corn Lily

Partridge Berry

YELLOW CORN LILY *Clintonia borealis*. Lily family *Liliaceae*.
   Flowers pale yellow, berries bright shiny blue. Height 6-16 feet. Rich woods.

PARTRIDGE BERRY *Mitchella repens*. Madder family *Rubiaceae*.
   Flowers twin, white or pink, becoming a single red berry at end of creeping stem. Height 3-6 inches. Woods.

BLUE-EYED GRASS *Sisyrinchium albidum*. Iris family *Iridaceae*.
   Flowers blue or white, leaves narrow. Height 4-24 inches. Sandy soil, open grassy places around lakes and ponds.

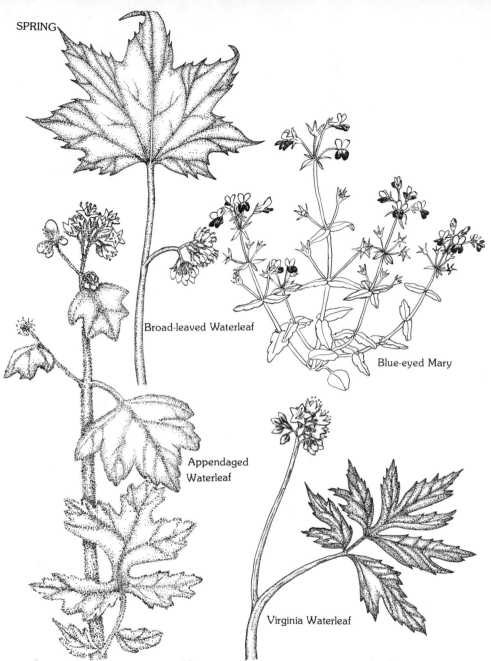

SPRING

Broad-leaved Waterleaf

Blue-eyed Mary

Appendaged
Waterleaf

Virginia Waterleaf

BROAD-LEAVED WATERLEAF *Hydrophyllum canadense.* Waterleaf family *Hydrophyllaceae.*
Flowers white to pink, leaves maple-like. Height 6-20 inches. Rich woods.

APPENDAGED WATERLEAF *Hydrophyllum appendiculatum.* Waterleaf family *Hydrophyllaceae.*
Flowers lavender-blue, stem and leaves hairy. Height 1-2 feet. Rich woods.

VIRGINIA WATERLEAF *Hydrophyllum virginianum.* Waterleaf family *Hydrophyllaceae.*
Flowers lavender-blue, leaves often marked as if stained with water. Height 1-3 feet. Rich
woods.

BLUE-EYED MARY *Collinsia verna.* Figwort family *Scrophulariaceae.*
Flowers with upper petals light blue, lower ones dark blue. Height 6-24 inches. Rich woods.

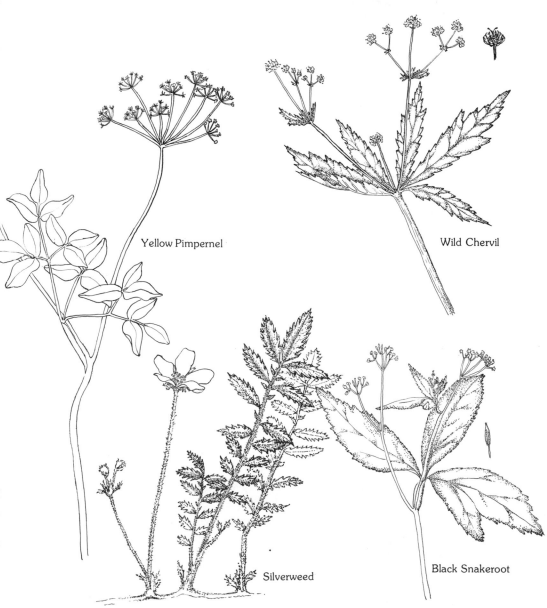

Yellow Pimpernel

Wild Chervil

Silverweed

Black Snakeroot

YELLOW PIMPERNEL *Taenidia integerrima.* Parsley family *Umbelliferae.*
Flowers a bright yellow umbel. Smooth stem, compound leaves. Height 1-3 feet. Dry woods, rocky hillsides.

SILVERWEED *Potentilla anserina.* Rose family *Rosaceae.*
Flowers shiny yellow, underside of leaves silver. Height 1-2 feet. Wet sandy beaches.

WILD CHERVIL, HONEWORT *Cryptotaenia canadensis.* Parsley family *Umbelliferae.*
Flowers white, long narrow seed pods. Height 1-3 feet. Woods.

BLACK SNAKEROOT *Sanicula gregaria.* Parsley family *Umbelliferae.*
Flowers greenish yellow, tiny hooked seeds. Height 1-3 feet. Dry woods.

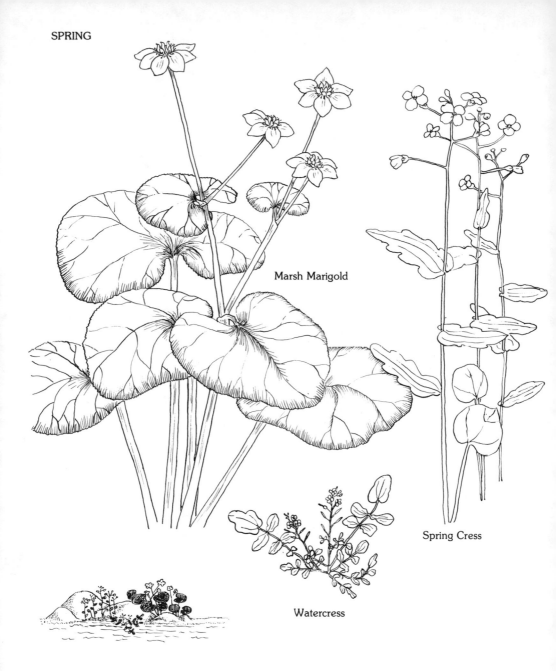

Marsh Marigold

Spring Cress

Watercress

MARSH MARIGOLD, COWSLIP *Caltha palustris.* Buttercup family *Ranunculaceae.*
   Flowers shiny yellow, leaves glossy. Height 1-2 feet. Wet woods, riverbanks, shallow water.

WATERCRESS *Nasturtium officinale.* Mustard family *Cruciferae.*
   Flowers white, leaves dark green, divided, edible. Height 4-10 inches. Grows in quiet streams.
   Alien.

SPRING CRESS *Cardamine bulbosa.* Mustard family *Cruciferae.*
   Flowers white, 4 petals. Height 1-20 inches. Wet places, stream sides.

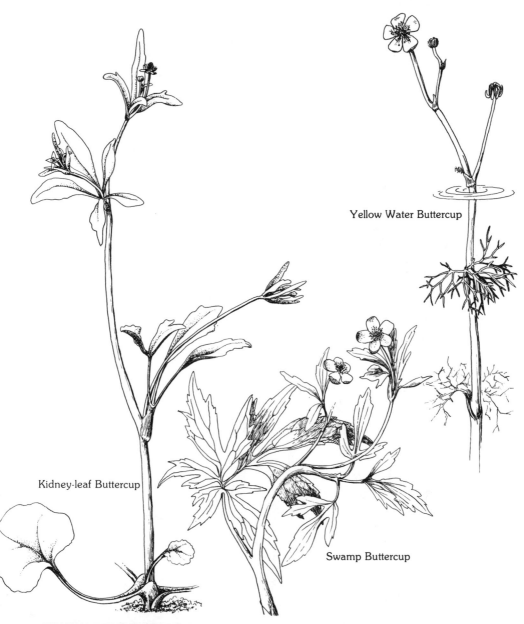

Yellow Water Buttercup

Kidney-leaf Buttercup

Swamp Buttercup

KIDNEY-LEAF BUTTERCUP *Ranunculus abortivus*. Buttercup family *Ranunculaceae*.
 Flowers small, inconspicuous, yellow green. Height 6-24 inches. Common in damp woods,
 roadsides.

SWAMP BUTTERCUP *Ranunculus septentrionalis*. Buttercup family *Ranunculaceae*.
 Flowers shiny yellow petals, succulent weak stems. Height 1-3 feet. Wet woods and meadows.

YELLOW WATER BUTTERCUP *Ranunculus flabellaris*. Buttercup family *Ranunculaceae*.
 Flowers golden yellow on branching stems above the water, submerged thread-like leaves.
 Height 6-8 inches. Quiet water, muddy shores.

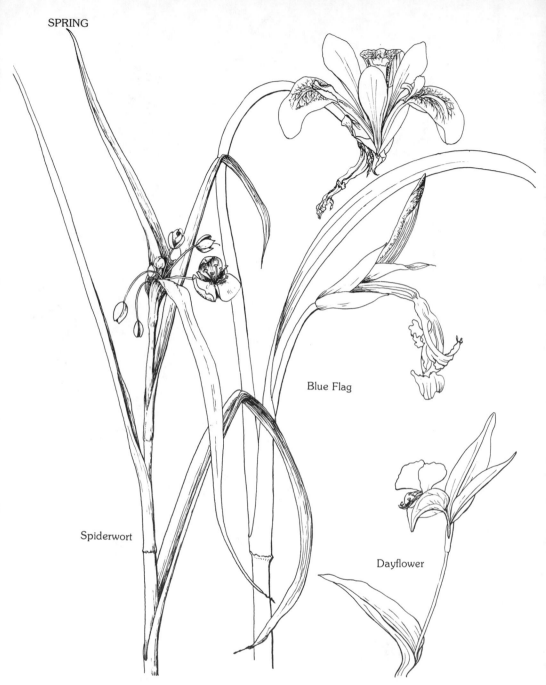

Blue Flag

Spiderwort

Dayflower

SPIDERWORT *Tradescantia ohiensis.* Spiderwort family *Commelinaceae.*
Flowers purple, sometimes rose, stem sticky. Height 1-3 feet. Prairies, open woods, roadsides, often cultivated.

BLUE FLAG, WILD IRIS *Iris versicolor.* Iris family *Iridaceae.*
Flower lavender. Height 1-3 feet. Marshes, edges of streams.

DAYFLOWER *Commelina communis.* Spiderwort family *Commelinaceae.*
Flower purple, white lower petal. Height 4-14 inches. Damp shade, often a garden weed. Alien.

Bearberry

Lupine

BEARBERRY *Arctostaphylos uva-ursi*. Heath family *Ericaceae*.
　Flowers white or pink, waxy, leaves paddle shaped, berries bright red. Height 4-8 inches. Trailing evergreen shrub, sandy or rocky soil.

LUPINE *Lupinus perennis*. Bean family *Fabaceae*.
　Flowers lavender blue in spike, leaves palmately compound. Height 1-2 feet. Sandy soil, open woods.

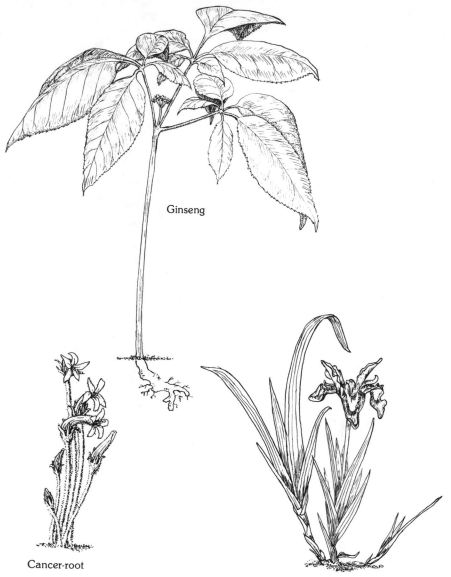

Ginseng

Cancer-root

Dwarf Lake Iris

GINSENG *Panax quinquefolium.* Ginseng family *Araliaceae.*
  Flowers green, leaves 5 parted. Height 8-24 inches. Woods. Rare.

CANCER-ROOT *Orobanche uniflora.* Broomrape family *Orobanchaceae.*
  Flowers white, stem hairy. Plant parasitic. Height 2-8 inches. Woods.

DWARF LAKE IRIS *Iris lacustris.* Iris family *Iridaceae.*
  Flowers blue. Height 2-3 inches. Only found in limy woods and shores of the upper Great
  Lakes Region.

Frostweed

Canada Anemone

Hoary Puccoon

HOARY PUCCOON *Lithospermum canescens*. Borage family *Boraginaceae*.
Flowers yellow, leaves hairy. Height 1-2 feet. Dunes, dry open woods.

CANADA ANEMONE *Anemone canadensis*. Buttercup family *Ranunculaceae*.
Flowers white. Height 1-3 feet. Wet fields, ditches, roadsides.

FROSTWEED *Helianthemum canadense*. Rockrose family *Cistaceae*.
Flowers yellow, single with 5 petals. Height 6-20 inches. Sandy, rocky woods.

Winter Cress

Hoary Alyssum

Shepherd's Purse

Pepper Grass

SHEPHERD'S PURSE *Capsella bursa-pastoris.* Mustard family *Cruciferae.*
  Flowers white, seed pods heart-shaped, cluster of basal leaves. Height 8-20 inches. Fields, roadsides.

HOARY ALYSSUM *Berteroa incana.* Mustard family *Cruciferae.*
  Flowers white, petals notched. Height 1-2 feet. Fields, roadsides.

WINTER CRESS *Barbarea vulgaris.* Mustard family *Cruciferae.*
  Flowers yellow, lower leaves lobed, clasping, with strong mustard taste. Height 1-2 feet. Turns fields and roadsides yellow.

PEPPER GRASS *Lepidium densiflorum.* Mustard family *Cruciferae.*
  Flowers white. Height 8-18 inches. Fields, roadsides.

Lousewort

Pussy-toes

Lyre-leaved Rock Cress

PUSSY-TOES *Antennaria plantaginifolia.* Daisy family *Compositae.*
   Flowers white, soft as a kitten's paw, plant fuzzy. Height 4-12 inches. Dry open fields.

LOUSEWORT, WOOD BETONY *Pedicularis canadensis.* Figwort family *Scrophulariaceae.*
   Flowers red and yellow, leaves hairy and fernlike. Height 1-16 inches. Sandy soil, dry woods.

LYRE-LEAVED ROCK CRESS *Arabis lyrata.* Mustard family *Cruciferae.*
   Flowers white, petals 4, basal leaves lyre shaped. Height 8-18 inches. Sandy soil.

By the middle of June, tree leaves are large enough to shut off the sun from the forest floor and the spring flowers. The summer flowers are found in meadows, old fields, the edges of ponds and woods, and along the roadsides. Daisies bloom everywhere. The freeways are white and blue with Queen Anne's Lace and Chicory.

WOOD LILY *Lilium philadelphicum.* Lily family *Liliaceae.*
Flower red-orange, facing upward and spotted near the base. Leaves in a whorl. Height 1-3 feet. Sandy soil, dry woods, prairies.

Angelica

Tall Meadow Rue

TALL MEADOW RUE *Thalictrum dasycarpum*. Buttercup family *Ranunculaceae*.
   Flowers whitish, male and female flowers separate. Height 1-5 feet. Ditches, wet meadows,
   streambanks.

ANGELICA *Angelica atropurpurea*. Parsley family *Umbelliferae*.
   Flowers white, stem purple, smooth and stout, leaves compound. Height 4-10 feet.
   Streambanks, swamps.

MICHIGAN LILY *Lilium michiganense*. Lily family *Liliaceae*.
Flowers red-orange, spotted upturned petals. Leaves in a whorl, plant tall and showy.
Height 3-6 feet. Streambanks, wet meadows, low spots.

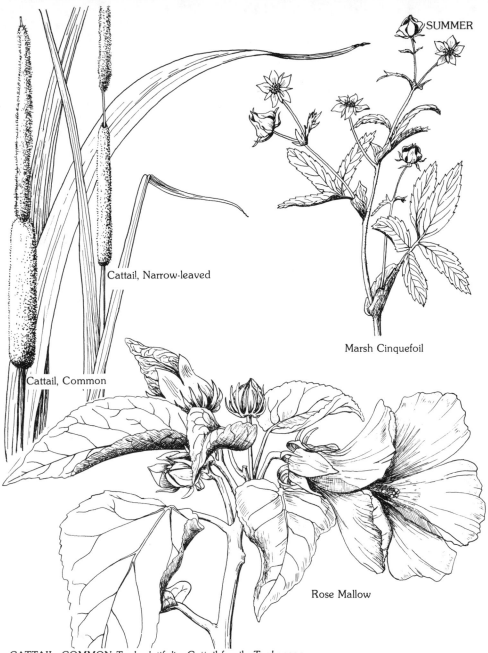

SUMMER

Cattail, Narrow-leaved

Cattail, Common

Marsh Cinquefoil

Rose Mallow

CATTAIL, COMMON *Typha latifolia.* Cattail family *Typhaceae.*
  Flowers a brown sausage-like spike. Height 3-9 feet. Swamps, ditches.

CATTAIL, NARROW-LEAVED *Typha angustifolia.* Cattail family *Typhaceae.*
  Flowers brown, male and female divided on stalk. Height 2-5 feet. Swamps, ditches.

MARSH CINQUEFOIL *Potentilla palustris.* Rose family *Rosaceae.*
  Flowers red-purple, sepals longer than petals, 5 to 7-fingered leaves. Height 8-24 inches. Bogs, swamps, stream banks.

ROSE MALLOW *Hibiscus palustris.* Mallow family *Malvaceae.*
  Flowers pink, large, showy. Height 5-7 feet. Marshes.

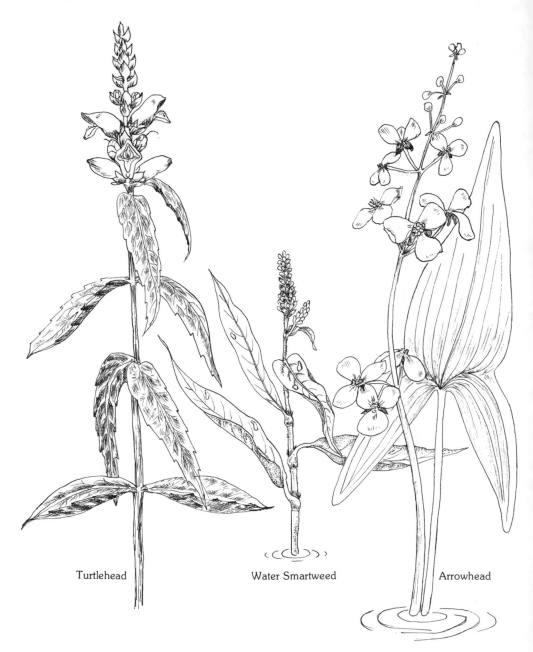

Turtlehead   Water Smartweed   Arrowhead

TURTLEHEAD *Chelone glabra.* Figwort family *Scrophulariaceae.*
  Flowers white, in profile resemble a turtle's head. Height 1-3 feet. Wet places, riverbanks.

WATER SMARTWEED *Polygonum coccineum.* Smartweed family *Polygonaceae.*
  Flowers pink. Height 1-3 feet. Shallow water, wet ground.

ARROWHEAD *Sagittaria latifolia.* Water Plantain family *Alismataceae.*
  Flowers white with 3 petals and large arrow shaped leaves. Height 1-3 feet. Pond edges,
  shallow water.

Fragrant Waterlily   Pickerelweed

FRAGRANT WATERLILY *Nymphaea odorata*. Waterlily family *Nymphaeaceae*.
 Flowers white 3-5 inches across, very fragrant. Leaves flat. Quiet water, ponds.

PICKERELWEED *Pontederia cordata*. Pickerelweed family *Pontederiaceae*.
 Flowers blue, leaves arrow shaped. Plants form beds at edge of streams, ponds. Height 1-4
 feet.

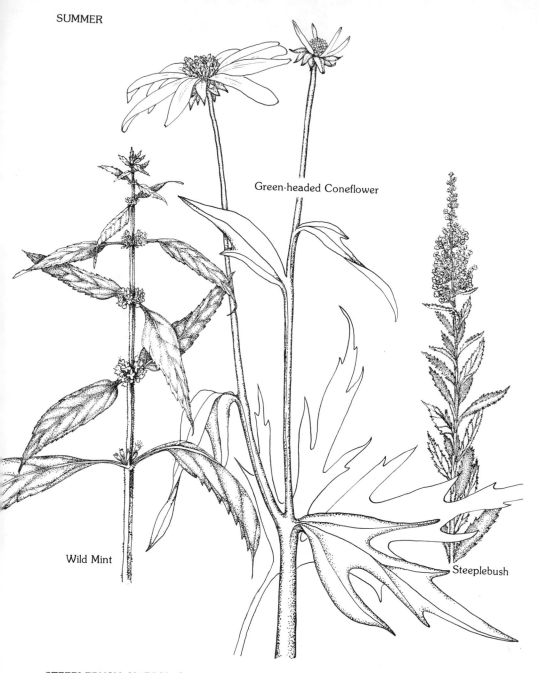

Green-headed Coneflower

Wild Mint

Steeplebush

STEEPLEBUSH, HARDHACK *Spiraea tomentosa.* Rose family *Rosaceae.*
Flowers pink. Undersides of leaves pale. Height 2-4 feet. Wet meadows.

GREEN-HEADED CONEFLOWER *Rudbeckia laciniata.* Daisy family *Compositae.*
Flowers yellow petals, green centers. Height 3-4 feet. Wet woods, streamsides.

WILD MINT *Mentha arvensis.* Mint family *Labiatae.*
Flowers white, lavender, stem square, leaves strong mint odor. Height 6-24 inches. Wet
meadows, woods, streamsides.

Purple Loosestrife

Spotted Jewelweed

Mad-dog Skullcap

MAD-DOG SKULLCAP *Scutellaria lateriflora.* Mint family *Labiatae.*
Flowers blue, seed pods resemble scullcap. Height 1-3 feet. Wet places, riverbanks.

PURPLE LOOSESTRIFE *Lythrum salicaria.* Loosestrife family *Lythraceae.*
Flowers magenta in a tall spike. Height 2-4 feet. Fills swamps, wet meadows, ditches. A garden escape. Alien.

SPOTTED JEWELWEED, TOUCH-ME-NOT *Impatiens biflora.* Jewelweed family *Balsaminaceae.*
Flowers orange to yellow, spotted, dangling on thin succulent stems. Height 2-6 feet. Wet, shady places.

Virgin's Bower

Water Pepper

Blue Monkey-flower

BLUE MONKEY-FLOWER *Mimulus ringens.* Figwort family *Scrophulariaceae.*
   Flowers blue. Height 1-3 feet. Wet woods, streamsides.

WATER PEPPER *Polygonum hydropiperoides.* Smartweed family *Polygonaceae.*
   Flowers white, greenish or pale pink. Height 1-3 feet. Shallow water, wet shores.

VIRGIN'S BOWER *Clematis virginiana.* Buttercup family *Ranunculaceae.*
   Flowers white, leaves 3 parted, climbing vine growing on river banks and in wet places.

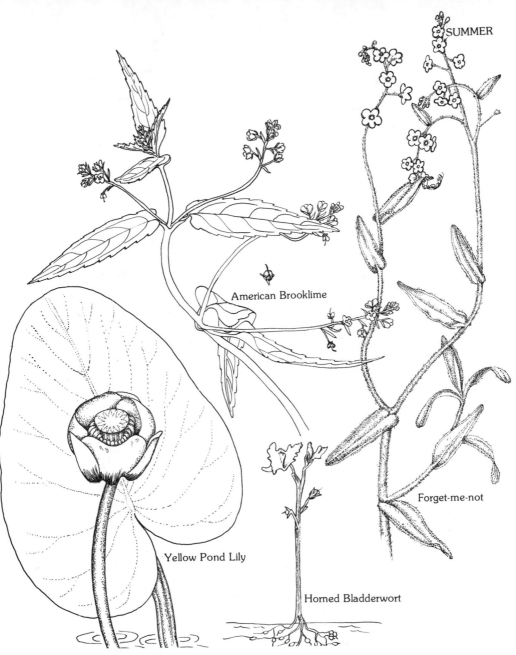

SUMMER

American Brooklime

Yellow Pond Lily

Forget-me-not

Horned Bladderwort

YELLOW POND LILY *Nuphar advena*. Water Lily family *Nymphaeaceae*.
   Flowers yellow, leaves erect above water, rarely floating. Height 2-6 inches above water. Quiet water, ponds, swamps.

AMERICAN BROOKLIME, SPEEDWELL *Veronica americana*. Figwort family *Scrophulariaceae*.
   Flowers blue, small. Stems and leaves smooth, succulent. Height 1-2 feet. Brooks and swamps.

FORGET-ME-NOT *Myosotis scorpioides*. Borage family *Boraginaceae*.
   Flowers blue with yellow eye. Height 6-24 inches. Grows in large colonies in wet places and shallow streams. Alien.

HORNED BLADDERWORT *Utricularia cornuta*. Bladderwort family *Lentibulariaceae*.
   Flowers bright yellow. Leaves submerged, threadlike. Height 6-10 inches. Wet muddy shores, bogs.

Cardinal Flower   Great Blue Lobelia

CARDINAL FLOWER *Lobelia cardinalis.* Lobelia family *Lobeliaceae.*
  Flowers scarlet, showy. Height 2-4 feet. Wet places and river banks.

GREAT BLUE LOBELIA *Lobelia siphilitica.* Lobelia family *Lobeliaceae.*
  Flowers deep blue with white stripes on lower petals. Height 1-3 feet. Wet places, swamps.

46

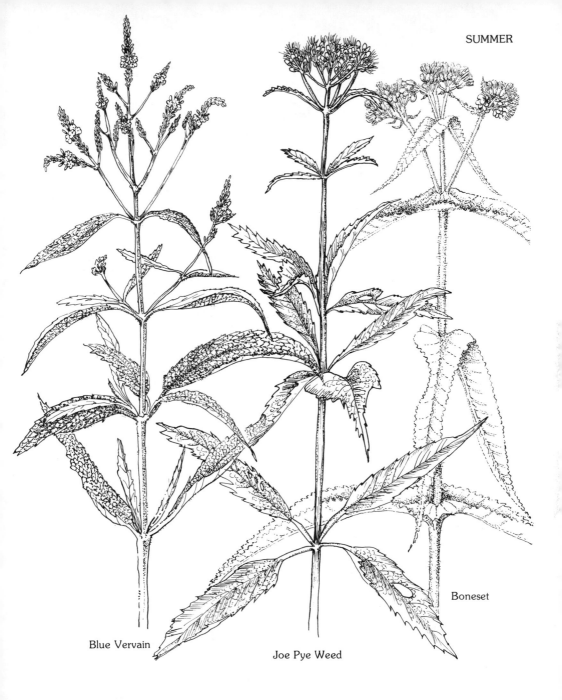

Blue Vervain

Joe Pye Weed

Boneset

BLUE VERVAIN *Verbena hastata.* Vervain family *Verbenaceae.*
 Flowers purple, in spikes, stems 4-sided. Height 3-6 feet. Wet, sunny places.

JOE PYE WEED *Eupatorium maculatum.* Daisy family *Compositae.*
 Flowers dusty pink. Height 2-6 feet. Wet, sunny places.

BONESET *Eupatorium perfoliatum.* Daisy family *Compositae.*
 Flowers white, stem pierces opposite hairy leaves. Height 1-5 feet. Wet, sunny places.

Nodding
Ladies' Tresses

Rose Pogonia

Grass-of-Parnassus

Grass Pink

NODDING LADIES' TRESSES *Spiranthes cernua.* Orchid family *Orchidaceae.*
Flowers small, white, spiraling around the stem. Height 6-18 inches. Bogs, edges of streams, wet meadows.

ROSE POGONIA *Pogonia ophioglossoides.* Orchid family *Orchidaceae.*
Flowers rose-pink, single. Leaf single. Height 4-20 inches. Bogs, wet mossy shores, old beach pools.

GRASS-OF-PARNASSUS *Parnassia glauca.* Saxifrage family *Saxifragaceae.*
Flowers white, petals with green veins. Spadelike bottom leaves. Height 8-24 inches. Wet limey places.

GRASS PINK *Calopogon pulchellus.* Orchid family *Orchidaceae.*
Flowers rose-purple, loose cluster of 3-15. Single leaf. Height 4-20 inches. Bogs, swamps, wet meadows.

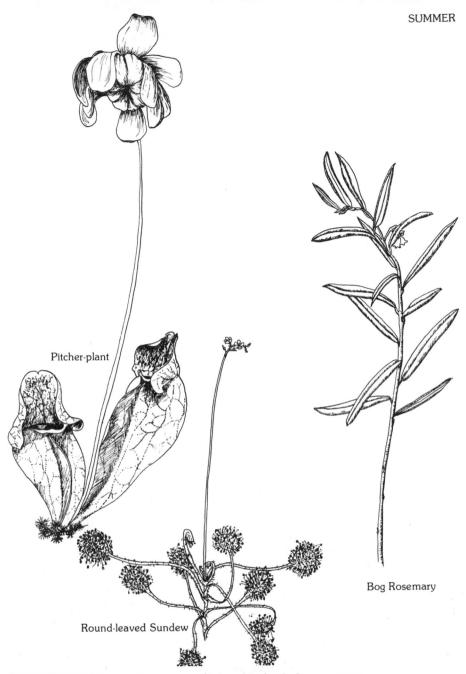

Pitcher-plant

Bog Rosemary

Round-leaved Sundew

PITCHER-PLANT *Sarracenia purpurea.* Pitcher-plant family *Sarraceniaceae.*
　Flowers dark purple-red. Plant carnivorus, traps insects in water-filled urn-shaped leaves. Height
　1-2 feet. Bogs.

ROUND-LEAVED SUNDEW *Drosera rotundifolia.* Sundew family *Droseraceae.*
　Flowers white to pink. Leaves have sticky hairs which catch insects. Height 2-8 inches. Bogs.

BOG ROSEMARY *Andromeda glaucophylla.* Heath family *Ericaceae.*
　Flowers pink, leaves leathery, aromatic. Height 10-20 inches. Bogs.

TICK-TREFOIL *Desmodium glutinosum*. Bean family *Fabaceae*.
Flowers pink on a slender stalk above a whorl of 3 parted leaves. Height 1-4 feet. Woods.

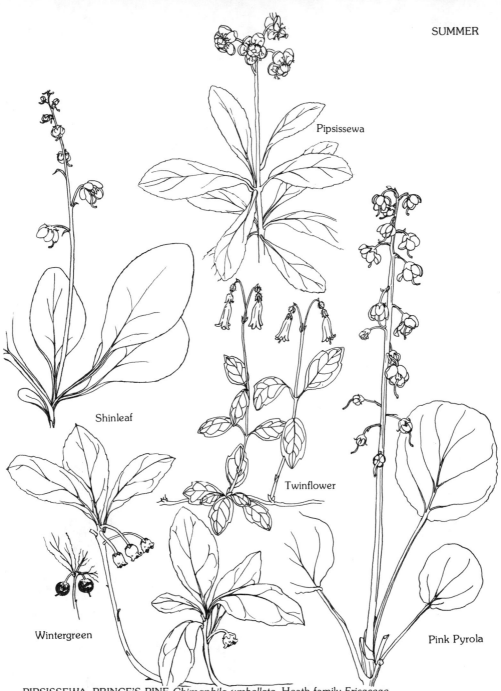

Pipsissewa

Shinleaf

Twinflower

Wintergreen

Pink Pyrola

PIPSISSEWA, PRINCE'S PINE *Chimaphila umbellata.* Heath family *Ericaceae.*
 Flowers a waxy pink cluster, shiny evergreen leaves circle the stem. Height 6-12 inches. Dry woods
SHINLEAF PYROLA *Pyrola elliptica.* Heath family *Ericaceae.*
 Flowers white, long curving pistils, oval leaves. Height 5-10 inches. Woods.
TWINFLOWER *Linnaea borealis.* Honeysuckle family *Caprifoliaceae.*
 Flowers pink, twin bells at top of slender stem. Height 3-6 inches. Cold woods.
WINTERGREEN, CHECKERBERRY *Gaultheria procumbens.* Heath family *Ericaceae.*
 Flowers white, waxy, bell-shaped. Thick shiny evergreen leaves, woody stem, bright red berries.
 Height 2-5 inches. Woods.
PINK PYROLA *Pyrola asarifolia.* Heath family *Ericaceae.*
 Flowers a waxy pink spike above rosette of rounded leaves. Height 6-15 inches. Rich woods.   51

Indian Pipe   Beechdrops

Pinedrops

Squaw-root

INDIAN PIPE *Monotropa uniflora*. Heath family *Ericaceae*.
  Flower and stem waxy white, rarely pink. Parasitic. Height 4-10 inches. Rich woods growing in leaf mold.

BEECHDROPS *Epifagus virginiana*. Broomrape family *Orobanchaceae*.
  Flowers and stem brown. Plant is a parasite on roots of beech trees. Height 6-24 inches. Beech woods.

PINEDROPS *Pterospora andromedea*. Heath family *Ericaceae*.
  Flowers white to reddish, bell shaped on brownish hairy stem. Height 10-18 inches. Dry soil under pine trees.

SQUAW-ROOT *Conopholis americana*. Broomrape family *Orobanchaceae*.
  Flowers and stem pale yellow-brown. Parasitic. Height 3-6 inches. Dry woods, oak forests.

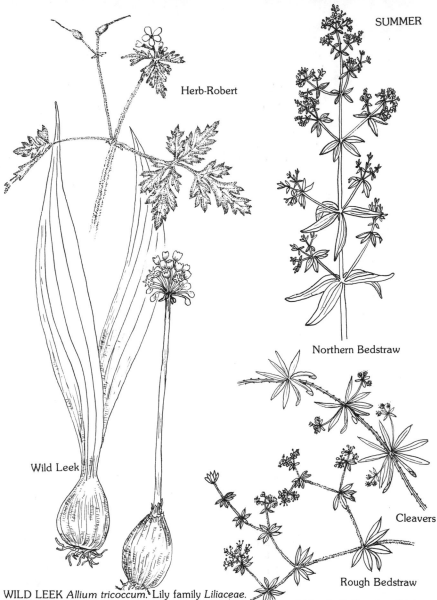

Herb-Robert

Northern Bedstraw

Cleavers

Wild Leek

Rough Bedstraw

WILD LEEK *Allium tricoccum.* Lily family *Liliaceae.*
Flowers white, bloom after the leaves appear. Onion scented. Height 8-18 inches. Rich woods in large colonies.

NORTHERN BEDSTRAW *Galium boreale.* Madder family *Rubiaceae.*
Flowers white, numerous in fragrant clusters, leaves in whorl of 4. Height 12-30 inches. Open woods.

CLEAVERS *Galium aparine.* Madder family *Rubiaceae.*
Flowers white, rough clinging stems, leaves in whorls of 6. Height 12-30 inches. Reclines on bushes in thickets.

ROUGH BEDSTRAW *Galium asprellum* Madder family *Rubiaceae.*
Flowers white. Long streamers, rough. Height 6-10 inches. Woods and thickets.

HERB-ROBERT *Geranium robertianum.* Geranium family *Geraniaceae.*
Flowers pink, leaves fernlike. Blooms all summer. Height 8-18 inches. Ravines, woods, gravelly shores.

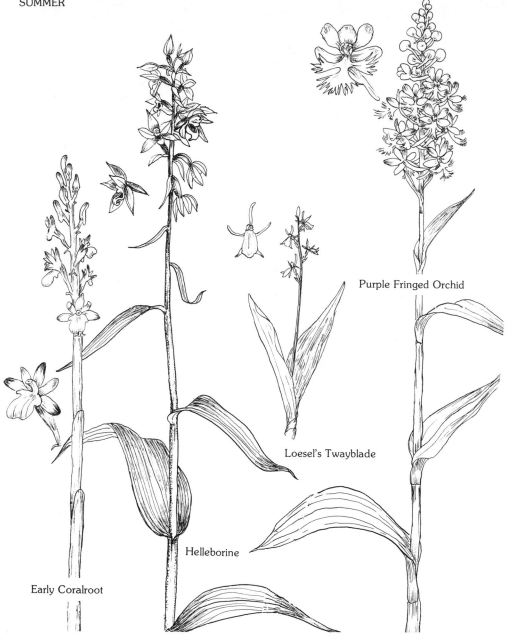

Purple Fringed Orchid

Loesel's Twayblade

Helleborine

Early Coralroot

EARLY CORALROOT *Corallorhiza trifida*. Orchid family *Orchidaceae*.
  Flowers pinkish, no leaves on stem. Height 8-20 inches. Woods.

HELLEBORINE *Epipactis helleborine*. Orchid family *Orchidaceae*.
  Flowers green tipped with purple. Height 1-3 feet. Woods. Alien.

LOESEL'S TWAYBLADE, BOG TWAYBLADE *Liparis loeselii*. Orchid family *Orchidaceae*.
  Flowers greenish yellow. Height 2-8 inches. Wet places. Rare.

PURPLE FRINGED ORCHID *Habenaria psycodes*. Orchid family *Orchidaceae*.
  Flowers pink-lavender with fringed lip. Height 1-3 feet. Swamps, wet woods, riverbanks. Rare.

SHOWY LADY'S-SLIPPER *Cypripedium reginae.* Orchid family *Orchidaceae.*
  Flowers pink and white. Beautiful and rare northern orchid. Height 1-3 feet. Swamps, bogs and
  wet woods.

Purple Gerardia

Fringed Loosestrife   Meadow-sweet

FRINGED LOOSESTRIFE *Lysimachia ciliata*. Primrose family Primulaceae.
Flowers yellow, nodding with fringed petals. Leaves paired with fringed stems.
Height 1-4 feet. Wet woods and riverbanks.

MEADOW-SWEET *Spiraea alba*. Rose family *Rosaceae*.
Flowers white, fragrant. Leaves lighter on underside. Height 1-4 feet. Wet meadows.

PURPLE GERARDIA *Gerardia purpurea var. parviflora*. Figwort family *Scrophulariaceae*.
Flowers pink-purple, leaves narrow, grasslike. Height 8-30 inches. Wet, sandy open places,
bogs.

Harebell

Fern-leaved False Foxglove

White Lettuce

FERN-LEAVED FALSE FOXGLOVE *Aureolaria pedicularia*. Figwort family *Scrophulariaceae*.
Flowers yellow. Fernlike downy leaves. Height 1-4 feet. Woods.

HAREBELL *Campanula rotundifolia*. Harebell family *Campanulaceae*.
Flowers violet-blue. Basal leaves round, upper leaves narrow, stems wiry. Height 6-18 inches.
Woods.

WHITE LETTUCE *Prenanthes alba*. Daisy family *Compositae*.
Flowers drooping clusters of white, pale green or lavender. Stem has milky juice. Alternate
leaves are a variety of cut shapes. Height 2-5 feet. Woods.

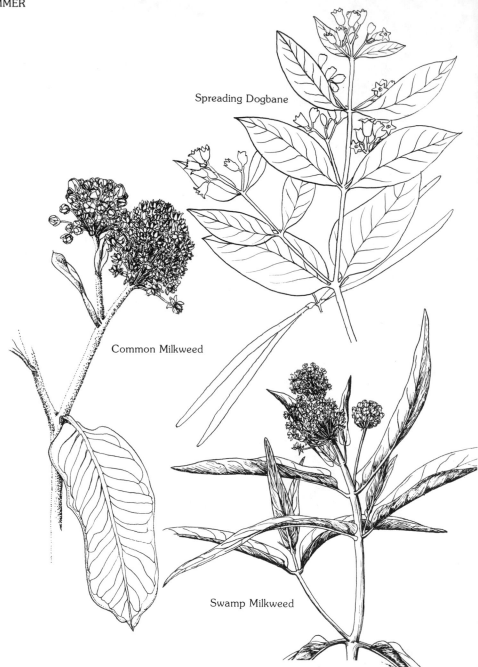

Spreading Dogbane

Common Milkweed

Swamp Milkweed

SPREADING DOGBANE *Apocynum androsaemifolium.* Dogbane family *Apocynacea.*
Flowers pale pink bells, long slender seed pods. Height 8-24 inches. Open dry woods.

COMMON MILKWEED *Asclepias syriaca.* Milkweed family *Asclepiadaceae.*
Flowers lavender pink, milky juice in stem, sticky. Height 1-4 feet. Ditches, riverbanks, wet
fields.

SWAMP MILKWEED *Asclepias incarnata.* Milkweed family *Asclepiadaceae.*
Flowers bright pink, milky juice in stem. Height 1-4 feet. Wet places, ditches, streamsides.

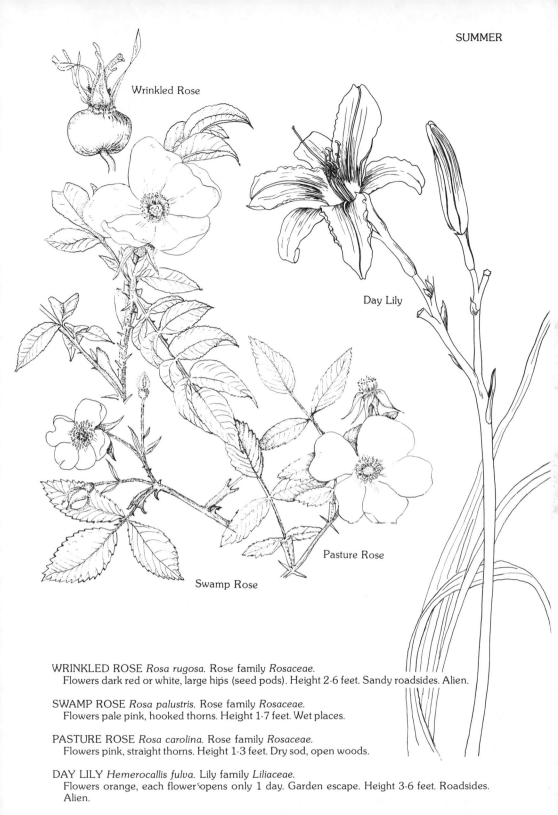

Wrinkled Rose

Day Lily

Swamp Rose

Pasture Rose

WRINKLED ROSE *Rosa rugosa*. Rose family *Rosaceae*.
  Flowers dark red or white, large hips (seed pods). Height 2-6 feet. Sandy roadsides. Alien.

SWAMP ROSE *Rosa palustris*. Rose family *Rosaceae*.
  Flowers pale pink, hooked thorns. Height 1-7 feet. Wet places.

PASTURE ROSE *Rosa carolina*. Rose family *Rosaceae*.
  Flowers pink, straight thorns. Height 1-3 feet. Dry sod, open woods.

DAY LILY *Hemerocallis fulva*. Lily family *Liliaceae*.
  Flowers orange, each flower opens only 1 day. Garden escape. Height 3-6 feet. Roadsides.
  Alien.

Butterfly Weed

Beardtongue   Indian Paintbrush   Bastard Toadflax

BEARDTONGUE, PENSTEMON *Penstemon digitalis.* Figwort family *Scrophulariaceae.*
  Flowers white or faintly violet, smooth opposite leaves. Height 2-4 feet. Fields, prairies, open
  woods.

BUTTERFLY WEED *Asclepias tuberosa.* Milkweed family *Asclepiadaceae.*
  Flowers brilliant orange, leaves fuzzy. Height 1-3 feet. Inland sand, dry prairies, open woods.

INDIAN PAINTBRUSH *Castilleja coccinea.* Figwort family *Scrophulariaceae.*
  Flowers in orange-red bracts. Height 1-2 feet. Dry meadows, prairies.

BASTARD TOADFLAX *Comandra richardsiana.* Sandal-wood family *Santalaceae.*
  Flowers white, small. Height 6-16 inches. Dry woods, prairies.

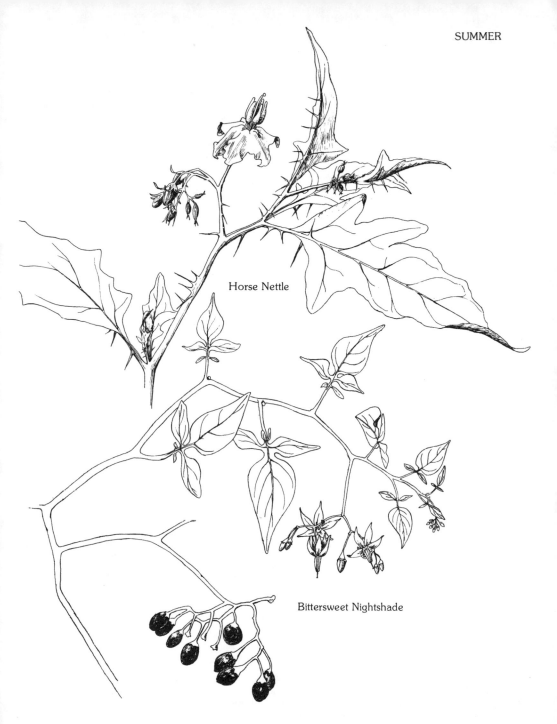

Horse Nettle

Bittersweet Nightshade

HORSE NETTLE *Solanum **carolinense***. Tomato family *Solanaceae*.
  Flowers white, berry yellow, plant spiny. Height 1-3 feet. Sandy soil, fields, roadsides.

BITTERSWEET NIGHTSHADE *Solanum dulcamara*. Tomato family *Solanaceae*.
  Flowers purple with swept-back petals. Yellow beak, berries green turning to red. Height 2-8
  feet. Disturbed ground, roadsides.

Horsemint

Sea Rocket

Tall Wormwood

HORSEMINT *Monarda punctata.* Mint family *Labiatae.*
  Flowers yellow spotted with purple. Stems square, strong odor. Height 1-2 feet. Dry sandy soil, dunes.

SEA ROCKET *Cakile edentula.* Mustard family *Cruciferae.*
  Flowers lavender, tiny. Stems succulent, fat seed pods. Height 6-12 inches. Sandy shores.

TALL WORMWOOD *Artemisia caudata.* Daisy family *Compositae.*
  Flowers yellow-green. Leaves tiny, narrow. Next year's flowering plant a cluster of silvery leaves. Height 3-5 feet. Sandy soil, dunes.

Yarrow   Wild Bergamot   Oxeye Daisy

YARROW *Achillea millefolium.* Daisy family *Compositae.*
Flowers white, fern-like, aromatic leaves. Height 1-3 feet. Dry fields and roadsides. Alien.

WILD BERGAMOT *Monarda fistulosa.* Mint family *Labiatae.*
Flowers lavender, stem square, strong mint odor. Height 1-3 feet. Woods, fields, roadsides, prairies.

OXEYE DAISY *Chrysanthemum leucanthemum.* Daisy family *Compositae.*
Flowers white, yellow centers. Height 1-3 feet. Common in fields and roadsides. Alien.

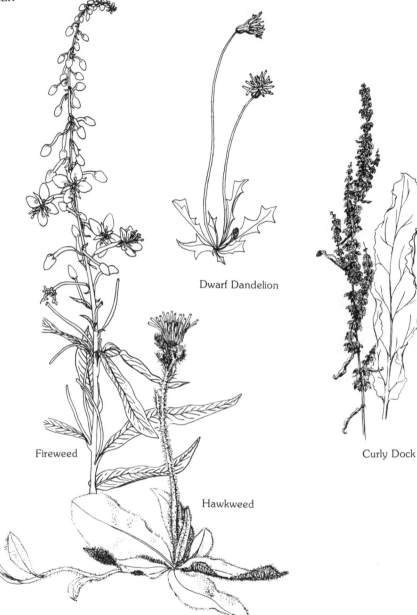

Dwarf Dandelion

Fireweed

Hawkweed

Curly Dock

FIREWEED *Epilobium angustifolium.* Evening primrose family *Onagraceae.*
  Flowers lavender-pink. One of the first plants to appear after burnings. Height 2-6 feet. Open woods.

HAWKWEED *Hieracium aurantiacum.* Daisy family *Compositae.*
  Flowers orange, very hairy plant, leaves basal. Height 8-24 inches. Fields, roadsides. Alien.

DWARF DANDELION *Krigia virginica.* Daisy family *Compositae.*
  Flowers yellow, one blossom per stem. Height 2-12 inches. Sandy soil.

CURLY DOCK *Rumex crispus.* Smartweed family *Polygonaceae.*
  Flowers green, seeds brown, winged. Height 1-4 feet. Fields, roadsides. Alien.

Spotted Knapweed

Sow Thistle

Prickly Pear

SPOTTED KNAPWEED *Centaurea maculosa.* Daisy family *Compositae.*
  Flowers pink-purple, resemble thistles but soft. Height 1-4 feet. Fields, roadsides. Alien.

PRICKLY PEAR *Opuntia compressa.* Cactus family *Cactaceae.*
  Flowers yellow, usually spineless, colonies. Height 2-8 inches. Rocks, dunes, sandy prairies.

SOW THISTLE *Sonchus arvensis.* Daisy family *Compositae.*
  Flowers yellow, leaves coarse, clasp stem. Height 2-5 feet. Disturbed ground, roadsides. Alien.

Chicory

Goatsbeard

CHICORY *Cichorium intybus*. Daisy family *Compositae*.
  Flowers blue sometimes white, close at noon. Height 2-4 feet. Common on roadsides. Alien.

GOATSBEARD *Tragopogon pratensis*. Daisy family *Compositae*.
  Flowers yellow, close at noon. Large seed heads, smooth stems. Height 1-3 feet. Common on roadsides. Alien.

Queen Anne's Lace

Field Bindweed

Hedge Bindweed

QUEEN ANNE'S LACE, WILD CARROT *Daucus carota.* Parsley family *Umbelliferae.*
  Flowers white, in seed flower cluster resembles a bird's nest, leaves finely cut. Height 1-3 feet.
  Common in fields, roadsides. Alien.

FIELD BINDWEED *Convolvulus arvensis.* Morning-glory family *Convolvulaceae.*
  Flowers white, trailing vine often forming tangled mats. Common in fields, roadsides, disturbed
  ground. Alien.

HEDGE BINDWEED *Convolvulus sepium.* Morning-glory family *Convolvulaceae.*
  Flowers white, pink, similar to Field Bindweed but larger flowers and indented leaves. Fields,
  roadsides, wet or dry.

Creeping Bellflower

Tall Bellflower

Common Mullein

TALL BELLFLOWER *Campanula americana*. Harebell family *Campanulaceae*.
Flowers blue, paler in the center. Height 2-6 feet. Woods.

CREEPING BELLFLOWER *Campanula rapunculoides*. Harebell family *Campanulaceae*.
Flowers blue, plant spreads by creeping runners. Height 1-3 feet. A garden escape. Roadsides.
Alien.

COMMON MULLEIN *Verbascum thapsus*. Figwort family *Scrophulariaceae*.
Flowers yellow, leaves soft and fuzzy. Height 2-6 feet. Roadsides. Alien.

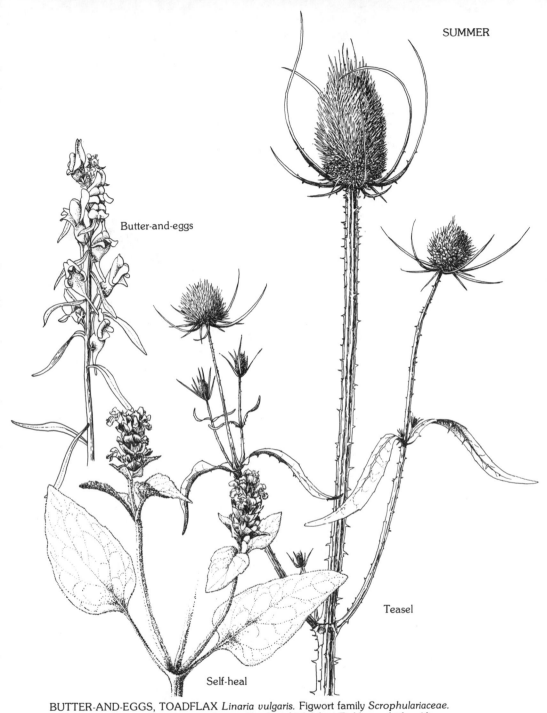

Butter-and-eggs

Self-heal

Teasel

BUTTER-AND-EGGS, TOADFLAX *Linaria vulgaris.* Figwort family *Scrophulariaceae.*
Flowers, yellow and orange snapdragon-like. Height 1-3 feet. Fields, roadsides. Alien.

SELF-HEAL, HEAL-ALL *Prunella vulgaris.* Mint family *Labiatae.*
Flowers violet, hooded, crowded, square stem. Height 3-12 inches. Roadsides, lawns. Alien.

TEASEL *Dipsacus sylvestris.* Teasel family *Dipsacaceae.*
Flowers pink on an eggshaped pincushion, stems spiny. Height 2-6 feet. Roadsides. Alien.

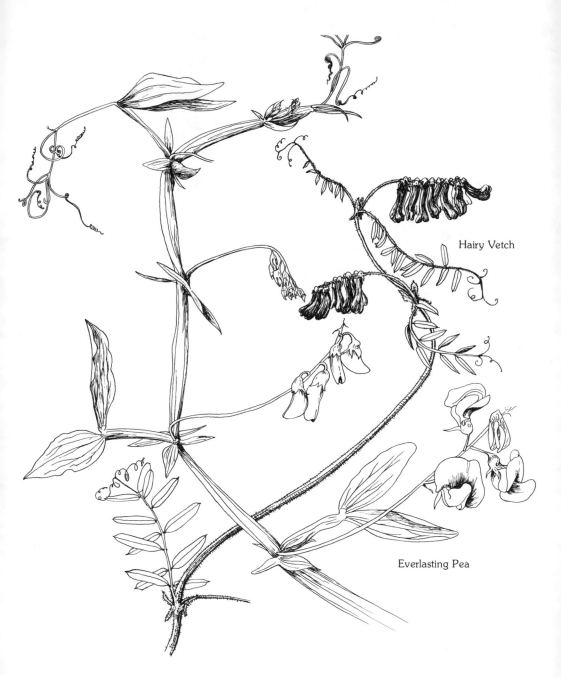

Hairy Vetch

Everlasting Pea

HAIRY VETCH *Vicia villosa.* Bean family *Fabaceae.*
   Flowers purple, sometimes purple and white, twining, vinelike. Height 1-3 feet. Fields, roadsides. Alien.

EVERLASTING PEA *Lathyrus latifolius.* Bean family *Fabaceae.*
   Flowers purple pink to white, winged stems, colorful. Height 1-3 feet. Fields, roadsides. Alien.

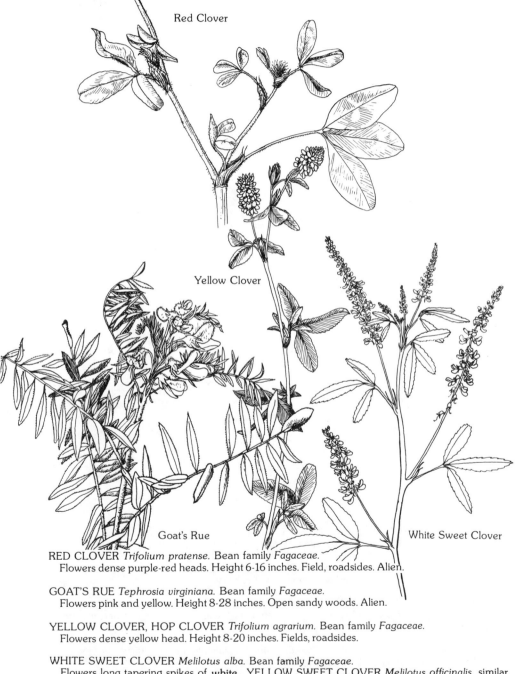

Red Clover

Yellow Clover

Goat's Rue

White Sweet Clover

RED CLOVER *Trifolium pratense*. Bean family *Fagaceae*.
Flowers dense purple-red heads. Height 6-16 inches. Field, roadsides. Alien.

GOAT'S RUE *Tephrosia virginiana*. Bean family *Fagaceae*.
Flowers pink and yellow. Height 8-28 inches. Open sandy woods. Alien.

YELLOW CLOVER, HOP CLOVER *Trifolium agrarium*. Bean family *Fagaceae*.
Flowers dense yellow head. Height 8-20 inches. Fields, roadsides.

WHITE SWEET CLOVER *Melilotus alba*. Bean family *Fagaceae*.
Flowers long tapering spikes of white. YELLOW SWEET CLOVER *Melilotus officinalis,* similar.
Height 2-5 feet. Fields, roadsides. Alien.

71

Black-eyed Susan

Viper's Bugloss

Evening Primrose

Lance-leaved Coreopsis

EVENING PRIMROSE *Oenothera biennis*. Evening Primrose family *Onagraceae*.
   Flowers yellow, quickly fade, many flowers, many leaves. Height 2-6 feet. Fields and roadsides.

BLACK-EYED SUSAN *Rudbeckia hirta*. Daisy family *Compositae*.
   Flower petals yellow, center brown, stem and leaves hairy. Height 1-3 feet. Fields, roadsides.

VIPER'S BUGLOSS, BLUE-WEED *Echium vulgare*. Borage family *Boraginaceae*.
   Flowers blue with long red stamens, plant very hairy. Height 1-3 feet. Fields and roadsides.
   Alien.

LANCE-LEAVED COREOPSIS, TICKSEED *Coreopsis lanceolata*. Daisy family *Compositae*.
   Flowers yellow. Height 2-3 feet. Dry sandy fields.

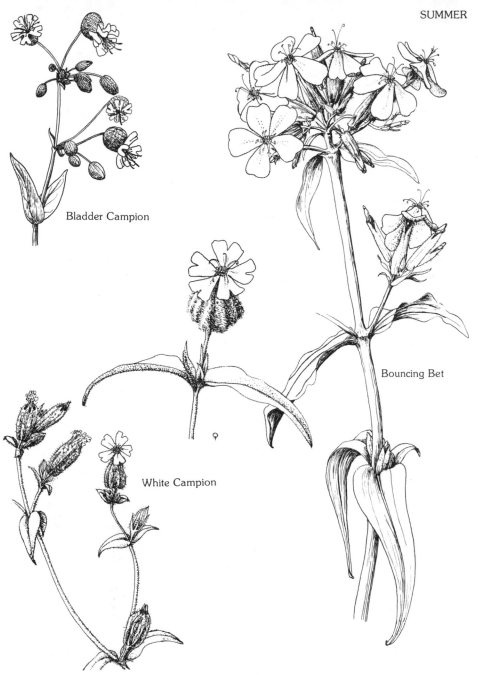

Bladder Campion

Bouncing Bet

White Campion

♀

BLADDER CAMPION *Silene cucubalus*. Pink family *Caryophyllaceae*.
　Flowers white, swollen calyx. Height 1-3 feet. Roadsides. Alien.

WHITE CAMPION *Lychnis alba*. Pink family *Caryophyllaceae*.
　Flowers white, open in the evening, male and female flowers separate, plant sticky. Height 1-3
　feet. Roadsides. Alien.

BOUNCING BET *Saponaria officinalis*. Pink family *Caryophyllaceae*.
　Flowers pink, white, many, fragrant. Height 1-3 feet. Roadsides. Alien.

Moth Mullein   Daisy Fleabane   Common St. John's-wort

MOTH MULLEIN *Verbascum blattaria.* Figwort family *Scrophulariaceae.*
  Flowers yellow or white. Height 2-6 feet. Fields and roadsides. Alien.

DAISY FLEABANE *Erigeron annuus.* Daisy family *Compositae.*
  Flowers white. Height 1-3 feet. Fields and roadsides.

COMMON ST. JOHN'S -WORT *Hypericum perforatum.* St. John's-wort family *Hypericaceae.*
  Flowers yellow with black dots on petals. Height 1-3 feet. Fields and roadsides. Alien.

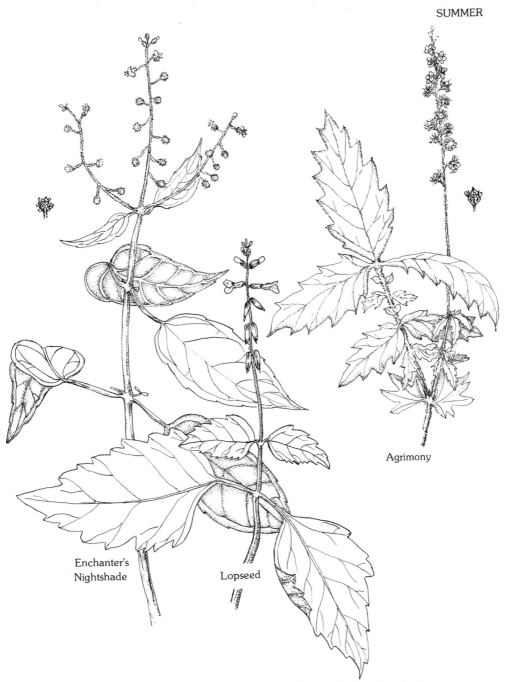

Agrimony

Enchanter's
Nightshade

Lopseed

ENCHANTER'S NIGHTSHADE *Circaea quadrisulcata.* Evening Primrose family *Onagraceae.*
 Flowers tiny pinkish-white, bristly hooked seed pods. Height 10 inches to 3 feet. Woods.

LOPSEED *Phryma leptostachya.* Lopseed family *Phrymaceae.*
 Flowers pink, seeds hang down. Height 1-3 feet. Woods.

AGRIMONY *Agrimonia striata.* Rose family *Rosaceae.*
 Flowers yellow, hooked seeds. Lower leaves divided into 5 to 9 parts. Height 1-6 feet. Woods.

In late August when fall arrives, the sky takes on a lavender hue and the wind blows from the north. The morning chill urges the teal to rise out of the marshes and fly south. Goldenrods begin to yellow the countryside. Asters bloom in every shade of blue to complement the brilliant fall colors of the Great Lakes woods.

White Snakeroot

Large-leaf Aster

LARGE-LEAF ASTER *Aster macrophyllus*. Daisy family *Compositae*.
  Flowers lavender blue, large basal leaves. Height 1-5 feet. Woods and clearings.

WHITE SNAKEROOT *Eupatorium rugosum*. Daisy family *Compositae*.
  Flowers white. Height 1-3 feet. Woods and clearings.

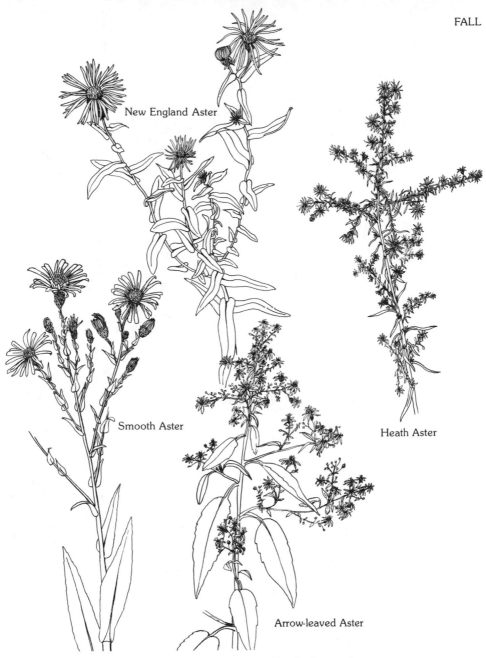

New England Aster

Smooth Aster

Heath Aster

Arrow-leaved Aster

NEW ENGLAND ASTER *Aster novae-angliae.* Daisy family *Compositae.*
  Flowers purple, leaves clasp stem, showy. Height 3-7 feet. Wet fields, prairies, often cultivated.

SMOOTH ASTER *Aster laevis.* Daisy family *Compositae.*
  Flowers blue or purple, leaves smooth, thick, blue-green. Height 1-3 feet. Dry open places.

HEATH ASTER *Aster ericoides.* Daisy family *Compositae.*
  Flowers white, small, many small leaves. Height 1-3 feet. Dry open places.

ARROW-LEAVED ASTER *Aster sagittifolius.* Daisy family *Compositae.*
  Flowers pale blue, lavender, or white. Height 2-5 feet. Woods, streambanks.

Woodland Sunflower   Flowering Spurge   Downy False Foxglove

WOODLAND SUNFLOWER *Helianthus divaricatus*. Daisy family *Compositae*.
   Flowers yellow with yellow centers. Plant rough, slender, with opposite leaves. Height 2-6½
   feet. Dry woods.

FLOWERING SPURGE *Euphorbia corollata*. Spurge family *Euphorbiaceae*.
   Flowers white, flat top of flowers above a whorl of leaves, juice of stem milky. Height 1-3 feet.
   Dry woods, fields, prairies.

DOWNY FALSE FOXGLOVE *Aureolaria virginica*. Figwort family *Scrophulariaceae*.
   Flowers yellow, lower leaves finely divided, hairy. Height 3-5 feet. Dry woods.

Pokeweed

Bristly Sarsaparilla

POKEWEED *Phytolacca americana.* Pokeweed family *Phytolaccaceae.*
  Flowers white, berries purple-black with red stems. Leaves large. Plant often grows in colonies.
  Height 4-10 feet. Damp woods, fields, fence rows.

BRISTLY SARSAPARILLA *Aralia hispida.* Ginseng family *Araliaceae.*
  Flowers white, berries purple. Height 1-3 feet. Dry open woods, sandy soil.

Saw-toothed Sunflower   Common Sunflower

SAW-TOOTHED SUNFLOWER *Helianthus grosseserratus.* Daisy family *Compositae.*
   Flowers yellow, leaves rough. Height 4-10 feet. Wet places, old fields, ditches.

COMMON SUNFLOWER *Helianthus annuus.* Daisy family *Compositae.*
   Flowers yellow with brown centers. Lower leaves heart-shaped, plant hairy. Height 3-12 feet.
   Dry fields, roadsides.

Bottle Gentian

Prairie Gentian

Fringed Gentian

Stiff Gentian

FRINGED GENTIAN *Gentiana crinita.* Gentian family *Gentianaceae.*
Flowers deep blue, 5 delicately fringed petals. Height 1-3 feet. Wet woods, streambanks.

PRAIRIE GENTIAN *Gentiana puberula.* Gentian family *Gentianaceae.*
Flowers deep blue, 5 petals, no fringes. Plant slightly downy. Height 1-2 feet. Prairies, dry open woods.

BOTTLE GENTIAN, CLOSED GENTIAN *Gentiana andrewsii.* Gentian famly *Gentianaceae.*
Flower petals closed, blue or dark blue. Height 1-3 feet. Wet woods, meadows, shores.

STIFF GENTIAN *Gentiana quinquefolia.* Gentian family *Gentianaceae.*
Flowers blue, tight clusters of tubular flowers, square stems. Height 1-3 feet. Wet woods.

Rough Blazing Star   Cylindric Blazing Star   Blazing Star

ROUGH BLAZING STAR *Liatris aspera*. Daisy family *Compositae*.
   Flowers purple-pink, set close to the stem. Height 6-30 inches. Sandy soil, dry open fields.

CYLINDRIC BLAZING STAR *Liatris cylindracea*. Daisy family *Compositae*.
   Flowers purple-pink, stem smooth, narrow leaves. Height 1-2 feet. Dry open fields.

BLAZING STAR *Liatris novae-angliae*. Daisy family *Compositae*.
   Flowers purple-pink, each on a short stem. Height 1-3 feet. Damp soil and dry open fields.

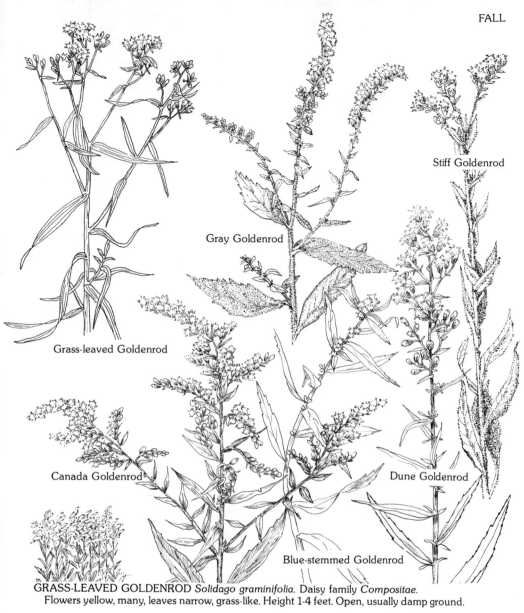

Stiff Goldenrod

Gray Goldenrod

Grass-leaved Goldenrod

Canada Goldenrod

Dune Goldenrod

Blue-stemmed Goldenrod

GRASS-LEAVED GOLDENROD *Solidago graminifolia.* Daisy family *Compositae.*
Flowers yellow, many, leaves narrow, grass-like. Height 1-4 feet. Open, usually damp ground.

GRAY GOLDENROD *Solidago nemoralis.* Daisy family *Compositae.*
Flowers yellow, rough gray-green leaves. Height 1-2 feet. Dry woods, sandy open places.

CANADA GOLDENROD *Solidago canadensis.* Daisy family *Compositae.*
Flowers yellow, plume-like. Height 1-5 feet. Grows in clumps in fields and roadsides.

BLUE-STEMMED GOLDENROD *Solidago caesia.* Daisy family *Compositae.*
Flowers yellow, in axils of the leaves. Height 1-3 feet. Woods.

DUNE GOLDENROD *Solidago spathulata.* Daisy family *Compositae.*
Flowers yellow. Height 1½-4 feet. Sandy soil, dry open woods.

STIFF GOLDENROD *Solidago rigida.* Daisy family *Compositae.*
Flowers yellow, clusters flat on top, leaves stiff, hairy. Height 1-5 feet. Dry fields, roadsides, prairies.

Rosinweed   Cup-plant

ROSINWEED *Silphium integrifolium*. Daisy family *Compositae*.
  Flowers yellow. Stiff opposite leaves. Height 2-4 feet. Prairies and roadsides.

CUP-PLANT *Silphium perfoliatum*. Daisy family *Compositae*.
  Flowers yellow, 2 upper leaves form a cup around the stalk. Height 4-8 feet. Open woods,
  prairies.

Prairie Dock

Compass Plant

PRAIRIE DOCK *Silphium terebinthinaceum.* Daisy family *Compositae.*
Flowers yellow, large basal leaves. Height 4-10 feet. Prairies.

COMPASS PLANT *Silphium laciniatum.* Daisy family *Compositae.*
Flowers yellow, leaves large, deeply cut. Height 4-10 feet. Prairies.

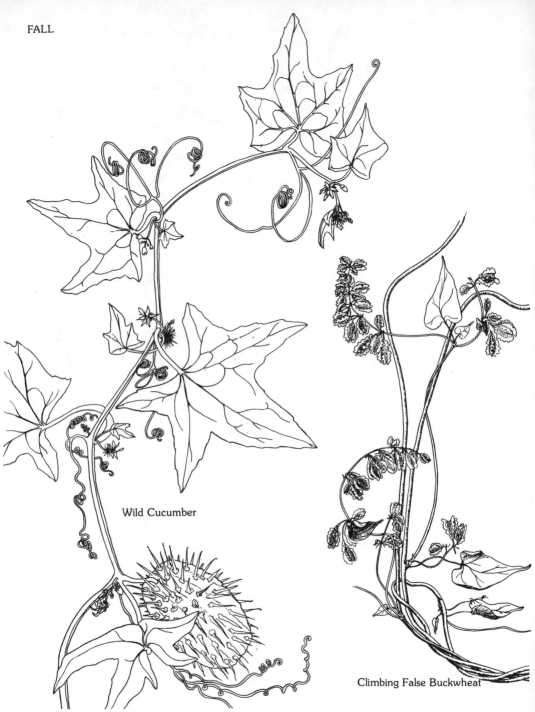

Wild Cucumber

Climbing False Buckwheat

WILD CUCUMBER *Echinocystis lobata.* Gourd family *Cucurbitaceae.*
Flowers greenish white, separate male and female flowers, fruit 2 inches long, soft prickly. Moist ground, thickets.

CLIMBING FALSE BUCKWHEAT *Polygonum scandens.* Smartweed family *Polygonaceae.*
Flowers white, green or pinkish and tiny, green winged seeds. Height 1-20 feet. Climbs over bushes in low wet woods and on streambanks.

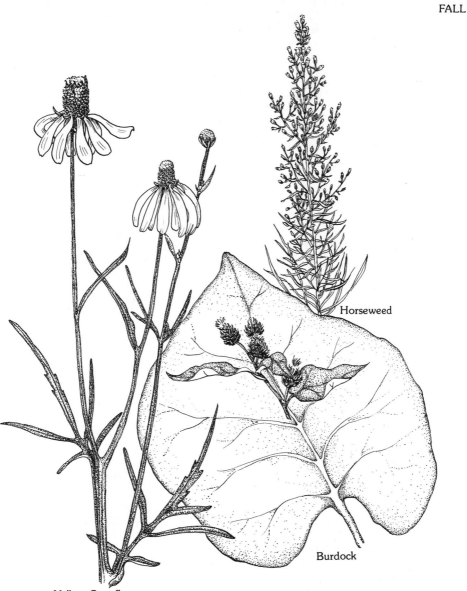

Horseweed

Burdock

Yellow Coneflower

YELLOW CONEFLOWER *Ratibida pinnata*. Daisy family *Compositae*.
   Flowers yellow, tall brown heads. Height 3-5 feet. Prairies, dry woods.

HORSEWEED *Conyza canadensis*. Daisy family *Compositae*.
   Flowers white, small, leaves many, slender. Height 1-5 feet. Roadsides, disturbed ground.

BURDOCK *Arctium minus*. Daisy family *Compositae*.
   Flowers purple, seed pods sharp hooked, large bottom leaves like elephant's ears. Height 1½ to 5 feet. Disturbed ground. Roadsides. Alien.

Sneezeweed

Ironweed

Tickseed Sunflower

Sneezeweed

TICKSEED SUNFLOWER *Bidens coronata*. Daisy family *Compositae*.
   Flowers yellow. Height 1-4 feet. Roadsides.

SNEEZEWEEDS. Flowers have yellow petals like skirts. Daisy family *Compositae*.
   If flower has purple center and narrow leaves, plant is *Helenium nudiflorum*. If flower has
   yellow center it is *Helenium autumnale*. Height 2-5 feet. Fields, prairies.

IRONWEED *Vernonia altissima*. Daisy family *Compositae*.
   Flowers purple. Height 4-10 feet. Wet fields and ditches.

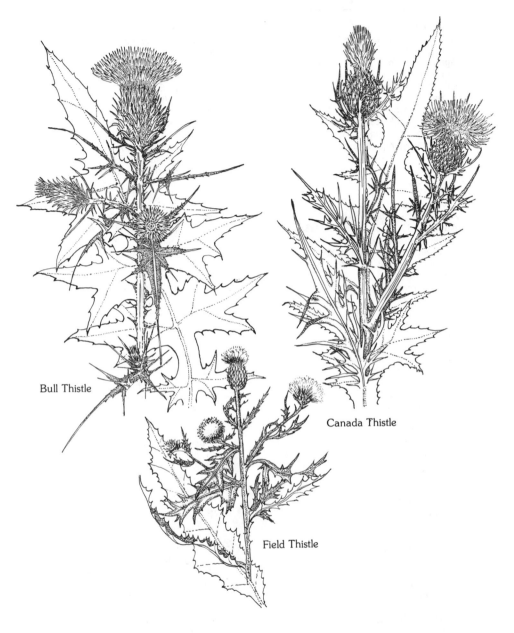

Bull Thistle

Canada Thistle

Field Thistle

BULL THISTLE *Cirsium vulgare.* Daisy family *Compositae.*
  Flowers purple-red, prickly wings on stem. Height 2-6 feet. Old fields and roadsides. Alien.

CANADA THISTLE *Cirsium arvense.* Daisy family *Compositae.*
  Flowers lavender, small, numerous, very common plant. Height 1-5 feet. Old fields, roadsides.
  Alien.

FIELD THISTLE *Cirsium discolor.* Daisy family *Compositae.*
  Flowers purple, undersides of leaves white. Height 3-9 feet. Old fields, roadsides.

References

Courtney, Booth, and James H. Zimmerman
1972 *Wildflowers and Weeds.* New York, N.Y.: Van Nostrand Reinhold Co.

Gleason, Henry A.
1974 (fifth printing) *The New Britton and Brown Illustrated Flora of Northeastern United States and Adjacent Canada.* New York, N.Y.: New York Botanical Garden.

Hanes, Clarence and Florence
1947 *Flora of Kalamazoo County, Michigan.* Portland, Maine: The Anthoensen Press.

Peterson, Roger Tory, and Margaret McKenny
1968 *Field Guide to Wildflowers.* Boston, Mass.: Houghton, Mifflin Co.

Rickett, H.W.
1965 *Wild Flowers of the United States, Part One, the Northeastern States.* New York, N.Y.: New York Botanical Garden.

Smith, Helen
1961 *Michigan Wildflowers.* Bloomfield Hills, Mich.: Cranbrook Institute of Science. **Bull. 42.**

Swink, Floyd
1974 *Plants of the Chicago Region.* Lisle, Ill.: The Morton Arboretum.

Voss, Edward
1972 *Michigan Flora.* Bloomfield Hills, Mich.: Cranbrook Institute of Science. **Bull. 42.**